Best Monday Inspiration

Best Monday Inspiration

Anthony L. Griffin

Master Trainer Services, LLC
1250 Scenic Hwy S
1701-298
Lawrenceville, GA 30045
United States of America
book@bestmondayinspiration.com
www.bestmondayinspiration.com

© 2021 Master Trainer Services, LLC
All Rights Reserved.
ISBN 978-0-9914115-0-4

IV

Contents

Introduction IX
Week 1 - Change .... - 3 -
Week 2 - Quality .... - 11 -
Week 3 – Potential... .... - 20 -
Week 4 - Do More Than You Think .... - 24 -
Week 5 - Be Amazing .... - 28 -
Week 6 - Imagination .... - 31 -
Week 7 - Perseverance .... - 35 -
Week 8 - Positive Energy .... - 39 -
Week 9 - Anything is Possible .... - 45 -
Week 10 - Develop .... - 49 -
Week 11 - Training .... - 53 -
Week 12 - Attitude .... - 55 -
Week 13 - Training .... - 59 -
Week 14 - Reinvent Yourself .... - 61 -
Week 15 - Perseverance .... - 63 -
Week 16 - Storms .... - 65 -
Week 17 - Being Acknowledged .... - 67 -
Week 18 - Know Thy Brain .... - 69 -
Week 19 - Your Heart .... - 73 -
Week 20 - Win First .... - 77 -
Week 21 - Do Not Fear .... - 81 -
Week 22 - Remembering Others .... - 85 -
Week 23 - Attitude .... - 87 -

Week 24 - Time ... - 89 -
Week 25 - Choices ... - 91 -
Week 26 - Subconscious Snack ... - 93 -
Week 27 - Freedom ... - 95 -
Week 28 - Best Work ... - 97 -
Week 29 - Motivation ... - 99 -
Week 30 - Make the Best Me ... - 103 -
Week 31 - Enemies ... - 105 -
Week 32 - Who You Are ... - 107 -
Week 33 - Acronyms ... - 111 -
Week 34 - Listening ... - 115 -
Week 35 - Infrastructure ... - 119 -
Week 36 - Publishing ... - 123 -
Week 37 - No Limits ... - 125 -
Week 38 - Core Message ... - 127 -
Week 39 - Detours ... - 131 -
Week 40 - Free Time ... - 133 -
Week 41 - Trauma ... - 135 -
Week 42 - Optimism ... - 139 -
Week 43 - The Best ... - 143 -
Week 44 - The Race ... - 145 -
Week 45 - Learning ... - 147 -
Week 46 - You Can ... - 149 -
Week 47 - Habits and Thoughts ... - 151 -
Week 48 - Thank You ... - 155 -

Week 49 - What a Ride .... - 157 -
Week 50 - Dreams .... - 161 -
Week 51 - Bunt or Out of the Park .... - 163 -
Week 52 - Lifelong Determination .... - 167 -

Best Monday Inspiration

Introduction

Without going into statistical detail about how difficult Monday mornings are for many people, let it suffice to say Monday morning does not have nearly the same appeal as Friday afternoon. **Best Monday Inspiration** is designed to bring a positive perspective to Monday and help you focus on pursuing your best all week long. The intent is to help you develop a modus operandi for how you think, how you make decisions, and how you strive to achieve things in all areas of your life. This is done by expounding on a quote every Monday in a way that inspires you to be and do your best. An **Inspiration Action** follows each quote so you can take that moment of positive thought and act on it throughout the week.

However, PLEASE don't take your action items and turn them into something that causes you stress! Make them small enough to comfortably complete in five or six days. Those small **Inspiration Actions** will add up over time and put you in a mode of regularly doing things that push you toward being your best.

One key item to understand is that being your best does not mean you simply become the best one day, and then that's it, race over, you've arrived. Being your best means constant growth and improvement. Being your best means you are continuously learning about yourself and the world while also working to make a consistently better impact on both.

Best Monday Inspiration is designed for individuals and teams. As an individual, it is designed for you to be a part of a virtual team in which each person is working to be his or her best. It is also designed for teams in companies, sports, families, or any group of people who are working together to produce some type of specific positive outcome. Team members can all be inspired in unison on Monday to be their best selves, individually and collectively making the **Best Team**, and ultimately, that's what allows them to have a better impact on the world. If you are a team leader, give copies to your team members, and use this as a weekly conduit to spark inspiration and positive energy for working together throughout the week.

This workbook contains 52 weeks of Best Monday Inspirations—enough to last one year. It's suggested that you take these inspirations one week at a time. Work with each inspiration like a cup of soothing hot tea that happens to last for seven days before it gets cold. After reading an inspiration, think it through, and dwell on ways you can apply it to you and your world throughout the week. Use it as a benchmark for making decisions and doing things differently than what you've done in the past. Most of all let it give you positive hope for the week, a true emotional feeling that says: "Things will be better. Move toward the best." Make a solid determination in your heart and mind that the week will be good, you will be successful, and you will overcome your challenges. If there is a failure, allow yourself to be inspired to get back up, learn from it, and keep moving forward to be your best!

Have a wonderful year, Team!

Suggestions for Success

Here are a few suggestions that will help you achieve the most success while completing this workbook

1. Schedule a weekly regular time to read and work on your weekly inspiration. Use your phone calendar, computer, whatever tool that will help you maintain a regular schedule for completing each week. Imagine yourself spending time every week completing the Best Monday Inspiration according to your schedule.

2. Keep the book with you. Study each weekly entry and refer to it as a manual to help you focus on the changes you seek. Remember - this is a workbook. Work it!

3. Notice the reoccurring themes. They are designed to help you revisit specific topics and see them from different angles and perspectives.

4. Each person and quote has been carefully selected. Research the person being quoted if you are not very familiar with him or her. Having background information about the quoted person will increase the impact of the inspiration.

5. Focus on your individual self. There will be topics that may tempt you to focus on the behaviors and thoughts of others, but your goal is to self-examine and produce change in yourself.

6. Don't complete the weeks and forget about them. Go back and re-read previous action items and continue integrating them into your life as appropriate.

7. Focus on the positive changes! There may be weeks where you don't complete all of the inspiration actions or you may feel you didn't hit the mark. Focus on the positive results, positive behavior changes and positive experiences and let that positive energy carry you through into the next week. For example, if you make a commitment to exercise 3 times in a week, but you only do it 1 time, don't focus on the two times you didn't exercise. Focus on the positive change that you did exercise once.

8. Have a Best Monday Buddy. It will be very beneficial to have someone to complete the book with. Find someone to partner with and hold each other accountable for completing each week. This might be one of the most powerful things you can do is to have a buddy system for completing this workbook.

9. Be relaxed. If you schedule yourself to complete your weekly inspiration on Monday at 3:00pm and you actually complete it on Wednesday at 8:00pm, it's ok. You can get back on schedule next week, but do your best to complete one inspiration every week. Also, we know that life happens. There may be times where you do miss a couple of weeks. This is where having a Best Monday Buddy helps to get back on track. The main goal is to finish the book in ~1 year and thoroughly complete each inspiration action.

Best Monday Inspiration
Week 1 - Change

There is beauty and power in change. Change is the device we have that can take us to the positive places we would never see if we stayed the same.

Let this first Best Monday Inspiration establish the reason we are here: **Change**. The purpose for spending your time and energy with this workbook is to take little steps toward changing from your current thoughts, behaviors, and habits to new thoughts, behaviors, and habits that are more in line with your true human potential.

Know and accept that **you can change**. It doesn't matter how or why you have arrived at your current thoughts, behaviors, and habits. We are all designed with the ability to change. We are not only designed to be able to change; we are also designed to excel. To excel, we **must** change and work toward our potential.

Finally, go ahead and change. Go ahead and live out your dreams. Go ahead and shift your thinking toward your limitless potential. You now have permission to surpass your previous life-speed limits and permission to break away from old thoughts and fears. It's ok. Go ahead. Change.

Have a wonderful week, Team!

Inspiration Action
Week 1 - Change

List three areas in your life that you would like to see changes in. For example, your job, social life, health, home life, relationships, finances, spirituality.

List six small actions that you can take to begin making changes in these areas. **These should be actions that can be completed in seven days or less.**

Example

My three areas that I would like to see changes in are finances, social life, and my job. My 6 small actions are:

1. Write down what I would like my finances, social life, and job to be in 5 years.
2. Have, or arrange to have, a conversation with someone who may have knowledge and experience that can help me achieve the changes I would like to have in my job.
3. Find and read an article or video that has information that can help me achieve the change that I envision in my finances.
4. Find and read information about jobs and social life in other cities.
5. Identify something that I do that negatively impacts me in these areas and write a plan to replace those behaviors.
6. Use social media to find a group that has a positive and relative focus on the items I am seeking change in.

Inspiration Action
Week 1 - Change

Using the example on the previous page, write your three areas and six small actions.

Inspiration Action
Week 1 - Change

Select one or two small actions from the list on the previous page. Remember that these should be actions that you can complete this week. Write your two actions on the next page and include specific days and times you will work to complete them this week.

> Example:
> 1. Have, or arrange to have, a conversation with someone who may have knowledge and experience that can help me achieve the changes I would like to have in my job.
>
>   Thursday, 8:00 p.m., I will post a request to social media asking to be connected to someone who has at least 5 years of experience in the job that I would like to be in 5 years from today.
>
> 2. Find and read an article or video that has information that can help me achieve the change that I envision in my finances.
>
>   Tuesday, from 7:00 p.m. to 8:00 p.m., I will find an article on the internet related to "best personal finance habits". I will print and read the article during lunchtime in order to do something different with my time and help me begin changing my financial thought patterns.

Inspiration Action
Week 1 - Change

Use the space below to write your two actions and include specific days and times you will work to complete them this week. Use the example on the previous page to guide you.

Inspiration Action
Week 1 - Change

Before next Monday, write what you did, the results, and your feelings about the outcomes.

> Example:
>
> I got home late Thursday, so I didn't make the post at 8:00 p.m. I did get up early Friday and make the post. So far, everyone who has responded says they don't know anyone who has that kind of job, but they will ask around. I feel very good about this because a few people said they didn't know I was interested in that kind of work and they are glad to know so they can help. I feel like I did something that will benefit me later and I feel like my vision is serious now and not just a dream in my head.
>
> I printed and read an article about personal finance habits called "Take myself to the bank". I read it at work and Jerry noticed what I was reading. He recommended a book that really helped him get his finances on track and mentioned a stock investment club his brother was thinking about joining. I feel like things could start moving too fast in this area, but I also feel like the information I have gained has already started a mental shift compared to how I was thinking about finances last week.

Inspiration Action
Week 1 - Change

Use the space below to record the details of your inspiration action. Write what you did, the results, and your feelings about the results. Use the example on the previous page to guide you.

Now that you've completed your first week of inspiration actions, look for opportunities to complete the other small action steps you listed on page 5. Remember to make them date and time specific and simple enough to complete in one week.

As you go through each week, remember to make your inspiration actions date and time specific and look for opportunities to do the "leftover" extra action items. Also, remember to **focus on the positive changes** that you experience.

Best Monday Inspiration
Week 2 - Quality

"You want people praising to others about owning your product or service, not just not complaining."
- Bill Scherkenbach

When an organization interacts with customers, is it enough for customers to "not complain?" As you interact in areas of your life, as a parent, coach, spouse, significant other, volunteer, teammate, employee, or boss, would no complaints from those you serve be all that you hope to achieve? While we can't expect every single "customer" to do summersaults when we have given our best, what should our goal be? We should make it our goal that—as much as possible—deliver experiences that give our "customer" a lasting impression of good quality.

Have you ever experienced a restaurant, store, product, or service provider that frequently inspired you to tell others how good its product or service is? Have you noticed how it makes **you** feel good when you tell somebody else that a business gave you a good quality experience? Have you noticed how good it makes you feel to tell someone about the great things your spouse or significant other does?

It will now be our goal to provide this level of quality as much as possible in our lives. It will be a challenging path as we encounter hurdles that are out of our control and impact our ability to deliver the best quality products, services, and experiences. However, with purposeful intent and a willingness to change how we do business (as a company, club, team, family, or another group) we can be confident that we will get there. As with anything else, it starts with an idea. The idea is: Our customers will do more than simply not complain. Our dedication to giving our best will cause our customers to praise our products, services, and attitudes. We will be providing the best products and services throughout our day, from household chores to multi-million dollar corporate projects.

We will make this idea a reality by changing how we perform at work, at home, and in the community. We will change how we engage each other, our customers, family, friends, and others. During the next twelve months, we will focus on making changes that increase the quality of how and what we do so that we continuously move toward being the **Best**.

Have a wonderful week, Team!

Inspiration Action
Week 2 - Quality

Pick an activity that you are likely to spend time doing this week.

Examples:

- exercise
- written communication at work
- prepare meals
- spend social time with others
- work on a task at work
- work on a task at home

List four small actions that you can take this week to begin increasing the quality of that one activity.

Example

I am likely to spend social time with others outside of work this week. The four small actions that I can take to increase the quality of that time spent with them are:
1. I can focus on improving my listening skills.
2. I can ask questions to learn more about someone.
3. I can encourage someone who is facing a challenge.
4. I can lead a conversation about something positive and make sure everyone has an opportunity to share their thoughts about it.

Inspiration Action
Week 2 - Quality

Inspiration Action
Week 2 - Quality

Select one or two items from your list of 4 small actions, write them here, and then work to complete them this week.

> Example:
> The two items I'm going to work to complete this week are:
> 1. At the birthday party this weekend, I'm going to ask someone where they would like to live 5 years from now. This will give me an opportunity to learn more about someone.
> 2. If someone begins gossip or any negative/unproductive conversation with me, I will focus on asking solution-oriented questions or switch the topic.

Using the example above, write your two items below.

Inspiration Action
Week 2 - Quality

Before next Monday, write the two things you did and the results. Write your feelings about the fact that you completed the two actions, regardless of the results.

Example:
1. I met Tom for the first time and after the usual greetings, I asked him where he would like to live in 5 years. He asked me if I was in real estate. I said no, it's just a question to get to know you. He was a little surprised, but after thinking about it for a few seconds, he said he hadn't really thought about moving, but if he had a choice, he would possibly like to move to Colorado because he's always liked skiing but has never been able to really pursue it in Florida. I learned a little more about his interests and we had a good conversation about how he might start thinking about a possible move to Colorado. He thanked me for reminding him how much he liked skiing.
2. I was feeling good about the conversation with Tom and had good energy from having completed 1 of my inspiration actions. I wasn't ready to work on the 2nd action, but two people were standing near me complaining about the cake and some of the other food items. They asked me if I liked the cake and I had to honestly tell them that I like sweets, so the cake was fantastic to me. I started thinking about how I could switch the topic and I asked them what was the best dessert they ever had. They both

stopped to think and then started talking about vacations they had gone on where they had great desserts. I was smiling to myself and thinking "Wow, it worked!" Normally, I would have just listened, hoping for it to stop, but since I had these inspiration actions in mind, I was able to do something different. I don't know if they realized what happened, but at least the negativity stopped for a moment and hopefully they'll realize the impact sooner a later.

I feel really good about having thought about this event before hand and having a mental plan with these inspiration actions and actually doing them. I had a little bit of anxiety when I arrived at the party as I wasn't sure how I would actually do them, but just having a mental plan really helped. The fact that I completed these inspiration actions definitely gives me energy for doing more inspiration actions.

Using the example above, before next Monday, write the two things you did and the results. Write your feelings about the fact that you completed the two actions, regardless of the results.

Best Monday Inspiration
Week 3 - Potential

"Ever since I was a child, I have had this instinctive urge for expansion and growth. To me, the function and duty of a quality human being is the sincere and honest development of one's potential."
- Bruce Lee

What do Mr. Lee and the **Best Monday Inspiration Team** have in common? Flying roundhouse kicks? Not quite, although we may feel the need to use them sometimes. The commonality between us is the understanding, belief, and pursuit of our full potential.

Why choose a martial arts icon from the 1970s to discuss potential? There was a significant amount of mental work and focus on potential that allowed Mr. Lee to obtain the extremely high level of martial arts performance he achieved. A few web searches will show you how much more than physical ability was behind his talent. His interviews reveal rare insight into the focused mindset of a superior achiever. Therefore, we are using him as an example because of his dedicated pursuit of potential and unwillingness to settle for status quo. This week I want to inspire you to pursue your **potential** by expanding, growing, and refining your knowledge and skills and have a focused mindset to be the **best**.

You were made to do great things.

Have a wonderful week, Team!

Inspiration Action
Week 3 - Potential

Take some time to think about and write down some "what if" scenarios. We're not asking you to do anything. Simply write about what it might look and feel like if you did do it and became successful at it.

Example:

What if I tried and became successful at:
- Taking up a new hobby I've been interested in?
- Writing a book, play, or movie?
- Getting a degree in a new field?
- Starting a new business?
- Trying a new sport?
- Playing an instrument?
- Starting a new friendship?
- Learning to cook?
- A new technical skill?
- Gardening?
- Painting?

Pick an example from the list above or from your own ideas. Write your what-if question and then write your answer to the "what if" question.

Inspiration Action
Week 3 - Potential

> Example
>
> What if I tried and became successful at writing a book?
>
> If I wrote a book and it became successful, that would feel satisfying because I've wanted to write a book for five years. It would be a historical work about the early nineteen-hundreds and the difference between technology then and today. I would enjoy speaking at public book readings and discussing other details that did not make it into the book. I would have a deep breath of relief at the end of the day when I come home and see my published book on my shelf.

Using the example above, write your own "what if" question and then answer it. The intent of this inspiration action is for you to create an emotional vision of doing something you're interested in. Include details such as:

- Why it would be important to you
- The impact it would have on you and others
- What obstacles you would have to overcome to complete it

Best Monday Inspiration
Week 4 - Do More Than You Think

"From the Marden (Dr. Orison Swett Marden) books I got not only the idea that I personally could succeed, but also the great truth that any man, yes every man, has in himself the capacity for success, if he will only use it."
- J. C. Penney

What keeps a person from using his or her capacity for success? There can be a number of things that deter a person from pursuing this great truth that J. C. Penney has expressed. Limitations that we place on ourselves often make up the list of things that prevent us from using the capacity of success each of us has. Becoming aware of these perceived limitations is the second step towards being able to use your individual capacity for success. What's the first step? Believe that you have the capacity for success.

A key detail about Mr. Penney's statement is that he sought to enable those around him to be successful–not just himself. He learned that since every person had this capacity, it was his duty to help others tap into theirs. In other words, he worked to be his best and helped those around him to be their best.

The main point is that regardless of your perceived obstacles, you can do more than you think you can do and you certainly can succeed in making your dreams come true.

Have a wonderful week, Team!

Inspiration Action
Week 4 - Do More Than You Think

Take some time to think about limitations that you put on yourself. Common examples are:
- Lack of education/knowledge/experience
- Current finances
- Relationships
- Negative self-perception
- What other people think and say
- Poor performance at work
- Family history
- Previous failures
- Fear of success
- Fear of failure
- What others have tried and failed

Take a piece of paper and write down the limitations that you thought of.

Look at your list. Are any of the items you listed **true, real, physical boundaries** that completely prevent you from using your full capacity for success? If not, draw a big X over the entire list. If you can safely burn it, burn it. If not, crumple it up and through it in the trash. This is an emotionally significant way of telling yourself that these things will not deter you.

Inspiration Action
Week 4 - Do More Than You Think

What do you think would happen if you looked at everything you listed and then tried to be successful at something that your list tells you that you can't be successful at?

Write your detailed thoughts about what you think would happen if you moved forward to accomplish something with the belief that you have the capacity for success in you. Take some time to ponder and visualize the possibilities of positive results.

> Example
>
> If I moved forward with starting my own restaurant even though I don't have a college degree, my first thought is that I would fail. If I move forward with the belief that I have the capacity for success in me and realize that there is nothing physically stopping me, I could take business classes online and prepare myself to be successful. It may take a long time to get it started, but if I stick with it, I can make it happen just like other people have made their dreams come true.

Using the example above, write what you think would happen if you moved forward and tried to be successful at something your list of limitations tells you that you can't be successful at.

Best Monday Inspiration
Week 5 - Be Amazing

"Don't be afraid to **be amazing**."
- Andy Offutt Irwin

Granted. We definitely will have some non-amazing moments (e.g. responding to unexpected difficulties, waking up in the morning). However, when it comes to what is important to us, such as the goals we have set, there is an opportunity to **be amazing**.

In the pursuit of being your **Best Self**, do not be afraid to be amazing. There will be obstacles and challenges that scream back the words "impossible; too much work; too many obstacles; why not just do it like everyone else; it's not worth it," and many other versions of fear, anxiety, doubt, and disbelief of being amazing. However, decide to do the amazing anyway.

- **Think amazing thoughts.**
- **Plan amazing solutions.**
- **Search** for and **create** the **amazing** even when you only see the non-amazing.

Let's read that one again.

- **Search** for and **create** the **amazing** even when you only see the non-**amazing**.
- **Think persistently** about being **amazing**.
- **Set the course** of your **attitude** toward **amazing**.

Best Monday Inspiration
Week 5 - Be Amazing

Believe it or not, that list represents the hard part, which is establishing a thought process dedicated to being amazing. The actual work of completing the tasks for your goals won't be easy, but it will be *easier* after establishing this thought process because we usually end up at the destination that we program into our internal GPS (Goal-Achieving Positioning System).

Have a wonderful week, Team!

Inspiration Action
Week 5 - Be Amazing

Do two small, but amazing, things for yourself and/or someone else this week.

Examples:
- Arrive 45 minutes early to an event and greet as many people as you can, including the staff.
- Bring someone breakfast.
- Finish something one to two days early.
- Propose an idea to someone. Keep your head up no matter how they respond and reward yourself for proposing the idea.
- Encourage three people.
- Find someone who you think is amazing and tell him or her so.

Write the two things you did, the results, and how you felt about what you did, and how you felt about the results.

Share your amazing inspiration actions on Facebook at https://www.facebook.com/bestmondayinspiration

Best Monday Inspiration
Week 6 - Imagination

"Imagination is everything. It is the preview of life's coming attractions."
- Albert Einstein

As science produces more information about how the brain works, the link between what we **envision** in our minds and what we experience in life becomes more understandable. As this link becomes clearer, it enables us to take advantage of the tools we have within us **to be our best.**

We know that imagining negative situations over and over again causes our bodies to react with stress—even before the situation actually occurs. A simple example is that some people can get headaches thinking about a possible negative interaction with a person before the interaction actually happens. Why is this? Because our brains cannot tell the difference between what is real and what is not real. Give your brain a thought and it will take the thought and run with it—whether the thought is positive or negative—and chemicals will be produced in your brain and body according to your thoughts. These chemical responses in your brain and body cause physical stress pains. We have been thoroughly trained to use our imagination for processing negative thoughts and possible negative outcomes, but for some reason, we have not been trained to use our imagination for processing positive thoughts and positive outcomes. That's what this week is about – using your power of imagination for your good!

Best Monday Inspiration
Week 6 - Imagination

Your brain is an arena waiting for you to fill it with your best thoughts, hopes, and aspirations, and in return, your brain will help drive you toward the goals you imagine. Of course, to achieve this, you will have to be persistent.

Here are a few ways to apply imagination:

1. When beginning a fresh new situation that has no negative experiences associated with it, you can take time to imagine your desired outcome before you get started and keep that picture as your goal regardless of what challenges come.
2. When faced with a situation that has real challenges and/or negative experiences already associated with it, analyze and process the reality of the negative things. Acknowledge their possibility. Then, apply **persistence** toward creating positive results. Keep your **attitude** in check (because that affects how your brain will work) and **keep moving forward**.
3. Imagine the positive result until it becomes a predominant thought and picture in your mind. Imagine the positive result frequently and intensely.
4. Avoid implementing a fear-based imagination. Implement an imagination based on what you hope for – not what you're afraid of. Implement an imagination based on the feelings of fulfillment and joy that you will have when your imagination becomes reality.

Best Monday Inspiration
Week 6 - Imagination

If you have imagined positive things for a long time and they remain just dreams, do not let them go. Continue to look forward to achieving them. There are so many stories out there of people holding onto what they have imagined until it came true as a result of taking action. You have the same tools within your mind that they have. Continue to imagine, continue to guide your thoughts toward being the best, and continue taking steps and doing the work to make it come true.

Have a wonderful week, Team!

Inspiration Action
Week 6 - Imagination

Write down two things you have imagined. You don't have to share these with anyone; it is only important that you see them on paper.

Examples of things you have imagined:
- An invention for making something better
- A dream relationship, house, job, or vacation
- A change in the way of life for a city, state, country, or planet
- An idea at work
- A debt paid off
- A new strategy for a sports team or club to try
- A new product
- A new service or business
- A healed relationship
- A new, better life for yourself

Write down your two imagination items and simply continue to picture them in your mind for the rest of the week. Imagine it consistently and intensely. Make it a predominate thought throughout the week. Imagine it deeply enough for you to feel excited about it.

Best Monday Inspiration
Week 7 - Perseverance

"I was born in Harlem, raised in the South Bronx, went to public school, got out of public college, went into the Army, and then **I just stuck with it**."

- Colin Powell

Sometimes success is simply **perseverance** –

- Putting your hands to the plow and not looking back
- Digging your heels in and refusing to give up
- Getting up more times than you fall down
- Starting with another piece of paper after throwing the previous one in the trash
- Continuing to hammer until the rock finally splits
- Continuing to knock until the door is finally opened
- Moving forward even if you have to crawl
- Always replacing "I can't." with "I will."
- Answering "It's hard." with "So what."
- Remembering the truth of perseverance as seen through the wonderful victories of others who have persevered

Have a wonderful week, Team!

Inspiration Action
Week 7 - Perseverance

Write one thing to which you were committed in the past and how it made you feel at the end of your accomplishment.

Write one thing that you've thought about doing in the future that would require you to stick with it. What would that look like at the end if you stuck with it and gave it your best?

Do something this week that requires you to stick with it. You can also look at the things listed in previous week inspiration actions and consider taking steps with 1 of those items.

Example:
Make an appointment that you've been putting off, such as a doctor, health spa, or massage appointment, or a tough conversation with someone, or anything that you have put off doing and you know you should have done it by now, or something related to what you have listed in week 3, week 4, or week 6.

Inspiration Action
Week 7 - Perseverance

Write what you did and how you felt about finally getting it done.

Best Monday Inspiration
Week 8 - Positive Energy

"I have nothing to do with negative relationships. I stay away from negative influences. I have no time for negative thinkers and pessimists. Such people will suck you dry until you have become just as pessimistic as they are. Then you'll have not just one but two losers."
- Arnold Schwarzenegger

This is a way of saying, "birds of a feather flock together," and you should have no part in a flock of pessimists. However, I think Mr. Schwarzenegger's version is a more concrete and necessary way of describing the effect of negative thinking, negative conversation, and negative energy.

There are different types and reasons for negative thinking, but there are two that cause the most harm:

- Thinking that comes from an individual who has disbelief and fear, which he or she spreads to others

- Thinking that comes from an individual who has incomplete information, only sees things from his or her own perspective, and then leads others to negative perspectives and wrong conclusions

Best Monday Inspiration
Week 8 - Positive Energy

Negative thinking, negative conversation, negative energy, and pessimism destroys and breaks down.

Positive thinking, positive conversation, positive energy, with balanced and factual feedback, builds up and brings life.

Everyone is free to choose which of these two mindsets to adopt. The critical factor in this freedom to choose is for a human being to **be** fully **aware** of the choice he or she makes, rather than responding to situations without realizing which mindset is being adopted.

What's the point? For a team to fully thrive at its **best,** there must be a continual, healthy, positive relational energy. As challenges will continue to occur, positive relational energy between team members is needed to successfully deal with challenges. Knowing who to discuss issues with and how to discuss them within the framework of producing **positive relational energy** will go a long way in helping the team be the best it can be.

Also, remember that human brains do not function as well with negative energy bouncing around inside. There's a neural–chemical reason for that, but that's another topic.

Best Monday Inspiration
Week 8 - Positive Energy

So let's flip Mr. Schwarzenegger's message:

I have everything to do with positive relationships. I stick close to positive influences. I make time for positive thinkers and optimists.

Such people will pump life into you until you have become just as optimistic as they are. Then you'll have not just one but two winners.

That's the absolute inverse.

The adjusted inverse is:

I seek positive relationships, positive conversations, and positive energy from those around me. I stick close to positive, successful influences. I make time for successful, positive thinkers and those who know how to encourage others while providing factual and actionable feedback. Such people will impart life to me, help me learn and grow, and become my **Best Self.** They will share their successes and failures to help me obtain as much success as I can and avoid failure as much as possible. Then you will have not just one person who is positive, successful, and pumping life into others, but you will have many human beings with this attitude.

Have a truly wonderful week, Team!

Inspiration Action
Week 8 - Positive Energy

Participate in one additional positive conversation this week, whether by starting one or finding one to participate in.

List four actions you can do to create more positive energy this week. It can be as simply as taking a break from negative news this week and looking for positive news sources. It could be calling someone to express gratitude or writing a thank you letter.

Participate in the additional conversation this week and complete two of the four actions you listed. Write about each of the three experiences, the results, and your feelings about completing these actions.

Best Monday Inspiration
Week 9 - Anything is Possible

One man swam the entire length of the Golden Gate Bridge, underwater, handcuffed, shackled, and towing air tanks on a 1,000-pound boat. He also swam the Golden Gate channel for one mile while towing a 2,500-pound boat. He paddle-boarded 30 miles/9.5 hours nonstop from Farallon Islands to the San Francisco shore. Handcuffed and shackled, he towed 65 boats filled with 6,500 pounds of wood pulp in Japan's Lake Ashinoko. Handcuffed and shackled, he fought strong winds and currents as he swam 1.5 miles while towing 70 boats, containing 70 people, in Long Beach Harbor.

These are just some of the things this man did. What's the kicker? He did all of this *after* the age of 60!

Who is he? Is he some TV show super Grandpa character? No. He is Jack LaLanne—the pioneer of modern fitness.

Jack is just one example of a human being determined to *exercise* his **amazing human potential** and to be his **best**. The previously mentioned stories are just a few of the physical demonstrations he became capable of after many years of pursuing his best. These capabilities came not just by building his strength but also from many years of persevering through what many told him shouldn't be done. You see, before Jack LaLanne, weightlifting was discouraged among athletes and other fitness-based occupations (police, firefighters, etc.).

Best Monday Inspiration
Week 9 - Anything is Possible

In some instances, pro athletes were even threatened to be fired if they lifted weights with Jack because it was believed at that time that weightlifting would negatively impact athletic performance. Think of those who not only believed that flying an airplane could not be done, but also those who insisted that even if flying an airplane could be done, it should *not* be done. It's unbelievable how the path of negative beliefs can be chosen in the midst of great opportunities.

While the rest of the world waited another twenty years to catch up to Jack's message of exercise and nutrition, Jack spent five years performing private research on weightlifting and nutrition. Then, in 1936, he opened the nation's first health spa, started what is known today as aerobics, and he developed the first instant breakfast meals, meal replacement bars, and some of the first workout machines, including the Smith machine and cable–pulley machines.

Jack started the first health and fitness TV show. Critics said it would be off the air in six weeks. They miscalculated slightly. It stayed on the air for more than 1,700 weeks and became the longest-running show of its kind in history.

It's real-life examples like this that drive me to continue to believe and to refuse to give up.

Best Monday Inspiration
Week 9 - Anything is Possible

And now for our quote:

"Anything is possible, and you can make it happen."

- Jack LaLanne

Have a wonderful week, Team!

Inspiration Action
Week 9 - Anything is Possible

Discuss with a friend, family member, or team member what you think could have been going through Mr. LaLanne's mind as he continuously approached things that no one had done before. What kinds of decisions did he possibly make in his mind that caused him to move forward and try what others would say is impossible?

Ask yourself this question, "What decisions do I need to make that will help me move forward in an area that I have been stuck?"

Write down your answers.

Best Monday Inspiration
Week 10 - Develop

"Let us develop the resources of our land, call forth its powers, build up its institutions, promote all its great interests, and see whether we also, in our day and generation, may not perform something worthy to be remembered."

- Daniel Webster, Secretary of State, 1841, at that time considered by some to be one of the greatest speakers of his day.

I hesitated using this quote because of its birth being rooted in politics and being from a somewhat controversial, though significant, historical political figure. However, every time I read it, it echoes a resounding call to superior action that should resemble our thoughts about our team. To explain and conclude, I'll offer you my interpretation:

Let us **develop** the internal resources of **our best selves**; call forth the abundance of individual and collective capabilities to **create our best team;** and build up our infrastructure, processes, and standards while promoting our great ideas. All of this will help us **provide** the **best service** and see whether we also, in our time here at this company, in this family, community, or team, may perform something outstanding, extremely valuable, cutting-edge, and worthy of being remembered.

Have a wonderful week, Team!

Inspiration Action
Week 10 - Develop

Write a short plan to develop something in your life—a plan to exercise, improve your diet, meet someone new, learn a new skill. This should be a simple activity and the plan and can be just a few lines.

Example: Plan to read a new book.
1. Spend 30 minutes researching books in your area of interest.
2. Pick the top three books that you find interesting. Have this step completed within three days of your start date.
3. Make a final selection based on reader reviews, availability, and price.
4. Purchase the book within five days of your start date.
5. Set aside 60 minutes a week to read until you've completed the book.

Use the next two pages to write your activity and plan, and to document your progress, results, and how you feelings about it.

Best Monday Inspiration
Week 11 - Training

"There is nothing that training cannot do. Nothing is above its reach or below it. It can turn bad morals to good, good morals to bad; it can destroy principles, it can recreate them; it can debase angels to men and lift men to angels. And it can do any of these miracles in a year—even six months."
- Mark Twain.

Wow, Mr. Twain took training to another level, didn't he?

I think he is actually saying that training is the foundation for changing your thoughts and behaviors into whatever you want them to be. In Week 1, we stated: "You can change." Training is a major part of that. If you want to do something that you are not able to do today—get trained. This includes technical skills, relationship skills, communication skills, or any skills. If it takes longer than Mr. Twain's belief of six months, keep training until you get the skill or behavior you desire.

Have a wonderful week, Team!

Inspiration Action
Week 11 - Training

Find and read an article about how your brain learns. Pick three interesting things from the article and write your thoughts about them.

Best Monday Inspiration
Week 12 - Attitude

"Our **attitudes** control our lives. Attitudes are a secret power working twenty-four hours a day, for good or bad. It is of paramount importance that we know how to harness and control this great force."
- Tom Blandi

Consider the popular power of a Hemi automobile engine. The design of a Hemi engine allows it to be one of the most powerful engines available for a street-legal automobile. Therefore, when the Hemi engine appears in streetcars, it produces many "oohs and ahhhs."

The attitude of a human being is like the powerful Hemi. It produces power for that person to propel forward or backward. When someone has a good Hemi (attitude) working under the hood, "oohs and ahhhs" are not far behind because of the forward-moving positive power that person produces and brings to the lives of others. When someone's attitude-Hemi is bad, it's like that wreck driving down the street, backfiring, smoking, and making onlookers stay far back so they are not exposed to the bad fumes.

The quote suggests that attitudes are a secret power. Let it remain a secret no longer. Become more aware of this power that drives you. Check your gauges (your responses to challenges) to see how your attitude-Hemi is running under the hood. Sometimes you have to tune up that attitude engine so it can produce all the positive power it possibly can.

Best Monday Inspiration
Week 12 - Attitude

Sometimes that attitude engine has to be totally taken apart and rebuilt to make it what it was truly meant to be.

So next time you see a Hemi, or any powerful, high-output engine, remember that you have one of those working 24/7 inside of you in the form of your attitude. If you make sure it's working positively on your behalf, you can cause "oohs and ahhhs" as you produce great things in your life and in the lives of others.

Have a wonderful week, Team!

Inspiration Action
Week 12 - Attitude

Write about a time when your attitude worked against you.

Write about a time when you recognized someone else having a bad attitude that negatively impacted you or a group.

Write about a time in your past when your positive attitude helped make a situation better.

Inspiration Action
Week 12 - Attitude

Look for opportunities this week to shift your attitude from negative to neutral to positive about something that is challenging. Write about your experience and how you felt about making that attitude shift.

Best Monday Inspiration
Week 13 - Training

"It's all to do with the **training**: you can do a lot if you're properly trained."
- Queen Elizabeth

"**Train everyone lavishly**, you can't overspend on **training**."
- Thomas J. Peters

Their insight into training is remarkable. Let's take these thoughts and inspire ourselves toward training in the areas that will help us be our best. Yes, training is a repeat topic because it is essential in your progress to being your best and working toward your potential.

Have a wonderful week, Team!

Inspiration Action
Week 13 - Training

For teams:

Discuss with your team a type of training program you could all begin together to help make your team the **Best Team**.

For individuals:

Find a short, authoritative training video online on a topic that you are interested in. Watch the video and write about what you learned and how you will apply what you learned.

Best Monday Inspiration
Week 14 - Reinvent Yourself

"Each of us has that right, that possibility, to invent ourselves daily. If a person does not invent herself, she will be invented. So, to be bodacious enough to invent ourselves is wise."
- Maya Angelou

Reinvent yourself continuously. Take yourself higher and higher. Don't settle for yesterday's you. When it comes to being your best, stale leftovers from years gone by just don't cut it. Make a **fresh, new, best you**! As you reinvent yourself individually, we will continue reinventing our team, our family, our department, our organization, and our club/group. We will continue changing the way we think and operate, inventing and reinventing ourselves into **the Best Team** we can possibly be!

Have a wonderful week, Team!

Inspiration Action
Week 14 - Reinvent Yourself

Write a description of a new you, using at least 50 words. Write the description as if you are already this person today.

> Example:
> I am a person who always arrives ten minutes early to scheduled events. I exercise twice a week, and I enjoy getting a good workout and burning calories. I manage my thoughts and emotions well. I seek to understand others first, and then to be understood. I spend quality time with my family and friends and continuously build healthy relationships.

Read what you've written three times a day for the rest of the week. Intensely imagine yourself doing everything you've written.

Best Monday Inspiration
Week 15 - Perseverance

"When everything seems like an uphill struggle, just think of the view from the top."

- Anonymous

In the midst of perseverance, sometimes the view becomes limited to the obstacles being faced. That's when discouragement and pessimism can set in. Human beings are designed to work by vision and imagination. By imagining the "view from the top" and holding onto the vision, you create a positive picture for your brain to pursue and propel you in subconscious ways toward your goal. That process will ultimately catapult you over or drill through the obstacles, and you will find yourself at the place you envisioned. Therefore, it is not enough to only not give up, but you must also constantly "look up" to the place you want to be. Therefore, the complete idea is: "Look up and don't give up."

Have a wonderful week, Team!

Inspiration Action
Week 15 - Perseverance

What is the view from the top for any struggles or challenges you are facing this week? Select one or two challenges that are on your plate this week. Then, write down what you would like to see as the final, best win-win situation for these challenges. Keep that description in mind as you face the challenges and work toward what you have described. At the end of the week, write your thoughts about your efforts to achieve the view from the top and how you feel about your results.

Best Monday Inspiration
Week 16 - Storms

"I am not afraid of storms, for I am learning how to sail my ship."
- Louisa May Alcott

This is a succinct reminder of our ability to master ourselves and determine how we navigate through the undesirable things that occur in life. The key to "learning how to sail my ship" is remembering that we have a ship. Although an individual may feel like he or she is drowning in the sea of difficult circumstances, the individual must remember that he or she has a ship that can be boarded and sailed.

Your ship will be as strong and capable of making it through the storm as you build it to be. Your ship is the sum total of your thoughts, gifts, talents, strengths, and weaknesses—including mental, emotional, intellectual, spiritual, and physical along with the environmental relationships you have created. Learning the depths, hows, and whys of all these parts of your ship is critical to being a good captain. After that introspective learning, you will know what changes to make to your ship to get the results you want, to then sail to the life destinations of your choice, making it through any storms that come.

Have a wonderful week, Team!

Inspiration Action
Week 16 - Storms

Write one or two things that you learned about yourself from your last storm. What caused you to feel less than positive and why? What interpretations and perspectives did you have that caused you to make the situation worse instead of better?

If this is your first time processing your own thoughts and behaviors to find what actions you have done to create your own storm (or make a storm worse), then, congratulations, this is a great day because you have taken the first step in having greater control of how you experience difficult situations.

If any storms come this week, stop and think about what you're doing and how you're feeling. Try to catch your thoughts and feelings and make a decision to either change your thoughts and feelings to something that helps make the situation better or at least be aware of your thoughts and feelings so you can then process and write what you discovered.

Best Monday Inspiration
Week 17 - Being Acknowledged

"There comes that mysterious meeting in life when someone acknowledges who we are and what we can be, igniting the circuits of our highest potential."
- Rusty Berkus

Happy Monday! I'd like you to meet YOU. Who are you? You are a brilliant individual who is working hard to take significant steps to be your best. You are wonderful and valuable, and you have something wonderful and valuable that the world needs. Even if you haven't discovered what it is yet, know that it is there—that's why you are alive—to give that wonderful and valuable something to the world.

It is my absolute pleasure to acknowledge whom you are (the best) and what you can be (continually better) as you continue down the path of your highest potential.

Have a wonderful week, Team!

Inspiration Action
Week 17 - Being Acknowledged

Write an introduction about yourself based on whom you believe yourself to be deep inside.

Write another introduction about yourself that you would like to be true one day.

Best Monday Inspiration
Week 18 - Know Thy Brain

"To **know the brain**...is equivalent to ascertaining the material course of thought and will, to discovering the intimate history of (your) life in its perpetual duel with external forces."
- Santiago Ramon y Cajal

It is said that for every action there is a reaction. I will add, in the context of human behavior, for every action and reaction, there is an explanation for why an action or reaction was chosen. Mr. Ramon y Cajal (recognized as one of the greatest neuroscientists of all time) explains where to find the explanations: To **know the brain** is to know the core reasons of what causes you to think the way you do and what determines (consciously and subconsciously) your actions.

Discovering the intimate history of your life and its perpetual duel with external forces suggests that the internal workings of your being are constantly reacting to things happening in the world around you. Your brain is executing billions of activities by the second and producing collections of intellectual, emotional, chemical, and physiological reactions in which the results are labeled as personality traits, behaviors, and habits.

Best Monday Inspiration
Week 18 - Know Thy Brain

Knowing how and why your brain is working the way it does in each situation provides a certain amount of awareness and the possibility of increased control over how you operate as a human being. "Why do I say what I say, and why do I do what I do?" is one of the most important questions for a human being to ask himself or herself. Even more important than that is to be able to answer that question for yourself in a meaningful and accurate way, understanding the make-up of your thoughts and will and changing your thoughts and will as needed to get the positive results you want in your life and the world around you.

Have a wonderful week, Team!

Inspiration Action
Week 18 - Know Thy Brain

Pay attention to what you say this week and take note when you say something that does not inspire you or others to be the best. Ask yourself, "why did I say that?" or "why did I use that tone of voice?" Write down your detailed thoughts about why. It may take some quiet time of contemplation and thinking through your personal history. The answer you are looking for will be about you, your thoughts, your memories, and perspectives. The answer would not be "because of what someone else said or did."

If you don't know what deep thoughts caused you to say or do it, then congratulations because you are about to experience the gift of learning more about your inner thoughts as your pursuit to your **Best Self** continues!

Best Monday Inspiration
Week 19 - Your Heart

"Throw your heart over the fence and the rest will follow."
- Norman Vincent Peale

What a dramatic twist to saying "put your heart into it." The fence represents the separation and challenges that exist between where you are today and where you want to be tomorrow. Today, you may not be able to immediately get your entire self over the fence into the land of accomplishment, but if you can hoist and hurl your heart over the fence, it will build momentum, and ultimately take the rest of your reality there. In other words, if you build enough enthusiasm, emotional energy, and determination toward what you want to accomplish, all of that will trigger the rest of what you need, and circumstances will change and eventually catapult you to completion.

Throw your heart over the fence and into the yard of being **your best** at whatever you want to accomplish.

Have a wonderful week, Team!

Inspiration Action
Week 19 - Your Heart

Write a short paragraph describing something that you've wanted to accomplish but have been hesitant to move forward with.

Describe why you have been hesitant to move forward.

Now, write a short paragraph describing how you can throw your heart over the fence (go all in) by moving forward with generating positive emotional energy about what you wish to accomplish. After studying what you've written, make a written plan to take the first few steps and document what happens.

Best Monday Inspiration
Week 20 - Win First

"Victorious warriors **win first** and then go to war, while defeated warriors go to war first and then seek to win."
- Sun Tzu

Hopefully, you have already set it in your mind that you are going to be successful in your goals and endeavors, with no "ifs," "ands," or "buts" about it. You've written your thoughts down, you've visualized what your success looks and feels like, and you are determined to make things happen. From this point forward, you will complete the actions that will give you victory in the things you want to accomplish. Of course, you will also persevere through the challenges that will come. Your behaviors and actions are driven by your subconscious thoughts. Win first in your subconscious, and then go to the battlefield and be victorious in all that you do.

Have a wonderful week, Team!

Inspiration Action
Week 20 - Win First

Write three things at which you want to win at this week and fill in all the details of what it would look and feel like for each win.

Pick one of the three things and do what you can to win at it this week and document your results.

Best Monday Inspiration
Week 21 - Do Not Fear

"I must not fear.
Fear is the mind-killer.
Fear is the little-death that brings total obliteration."
- Paul Atreides from the movie *Dune*

While this observation of fear comes from a Hollywood script based on a science fiction novel from the 1960s, I have found it to be a wonderful and poignantly accurate description of fear's effect on a human being attempting to reach his or her potential.

There are many different discussions about fear that could take place from this point, including the perspective that fear is necessary to ignite performance in some situations. The intent of this inspiration is not to discuss the caveats of fear. The intent of this inspiration is to call fear out, put it on the table, and dismantle it before it dismantles your dreams.

As you discover opportunities to pursue, find solutions to problems, and ponder "what if" scenarios in your professional and personal lives, you'll look at the possible paths you can go down for each opportunity. At this point, there may be a fork in the road in your mind. One way says "I/we can do it. I/we will find a way. It may be tough, but the vision of what I see can come to pass."

Best Monday Inspiration
Week 21 - Do Not Fear

The other way says "But… What if?… Probably not… No way…. That's crazy."

Here's the kicker, that point of analysis is a must. Analyzing for possible failure points is critical to success because you need to identify possible failure points so you can avoid them. However, when your mind sees the obstacles (hurdles, challenges, possible failure, and what you will feel or look like if you fail), there is an internal compass that points down one of those mental paths. If it is the mind-killing fear, you've just been defeated before you took the first step.

Fear is good for one thing. It is an alert that lets you know when you are out of your comfort zone. When you receive this alert, recognize it for what it is—an alert. It should not become a blockade to your progress. After receiving the alert, you may determine that some additional skill, knowledge, or practice may be needed to complete the task or goal. In that case, use the alert to take the needed actions. If, after receiving and analyzing the alert, you realize that there is no other preparation needed, and it's just a recognition of being out of your comfort zone, then it's time to become comfortable with the task or goal by doing it. You can manage your fear when you stop to analyze it, figure out what has triggered it, and address what it is communicating to you.

Best Monday Inspiration
Week 21 - Do Not Fear

What we usually hear when an alert comes is, "Hey, this is something you were unsuccessful at before, or you do not have enough proven success to know that you will get it right. For your own safety, I (fear) will wreak havoc in your head and prevent you from doing this lest you die. You'll thank me later for keeping you in your comfort zone and safe from those pesky dreams and ideas you have."

The more productive interpretation of the alert is "Wow. I haven't done this before", or "I had a bad experience with this in the past, but that doesn't mean that I can't or won't be successful in the future. I can tap into my human potential and be successful at this. It may take time and work, but each thing that I must do to be successful will increase my overall personal ability, pushing me further along in my overall success. Even if I do fail, I will survive and learn from this."

For further inspiration on managing fear and awakening to your full potential, check out the movie *Dune* (1984, 2021). There's a lot to be said in the movie regarding human beings carrying so much potential and not being aware of it even though we periodically exercise some of the traits and gifts of our capabilities.

Have a wonderful week, Team!

Inspiration Action
Week 21 - Do Not Fear

Discuss with someone that you trust one or two things that cause you fear regarding the goals you are working on. The one or two things can be work projects, personal projects, relationships, or whatever comes to mind. Tell the person what you're afraid of and why you're afraid. Tell him or her you're not asking for a resolution, rather only for an opportunity to express yourself and for them to understand. After you feel positive they understand, you can ask for one or two suggestions for resolutions (if you want).

Write down the one or two things that you plan to share with the person you trust.

After sharing, write down how you felt afterward.

Best Monday Inspiration
Week 22 - Remembering Others

"The brave die never, though they sleep in dust; their courage nerves a thousand living men.'
- Minot J. Savage

There are many that have gone before us, giving their best efforts and sometimes with great sacrifice. Past and present, their efforts encourage us to do everything we can with what we have been given while we remain among the living.

Have a wonderful week, Team

Inspiration Action
Week 22 - Remembering Others

Take a moment to remember those who gave their best to make room for you to give your best. Remember the efforts they gave as you give your efforts this week to be your best. They can be historical figures, family, friends, etc. Write their names here and what you remember. Consider sharing with your team.

Best Monday Inspiration
Week 23 - Attitude

"Any fact facing us is not as important as our **attitude** toward it, for that determines our success or failure. The way you think about a fact may defeat you before you ever do anything about it. You are overcome by the fact because you think you are."
~ Norman Vincent Peale

"Nothing can stop the man with the right mental **attitude** from achieving his goal; nothing on earth can help the man with the wrong mental **attitude**."
- Thomas Jefferson

I used to have a really bad attitude. I complained all the time, thinking that everybody everywhere was doing everything wrong. Work, church, stores, government, parties, playing sports, you name it, I was complaining about it. Eventually, I realized that complaining and having a bad attitude was getting me nowhere.

Although it felt appropriate to complain and I felt justified in my complaints, it just made the world seem worse and it held me in a state of no progress. Then one day, I was introduced to changing my **attitude**. Since then, my progress has continued to move forward and I began to see the plentiful opportunities that lay before me—opportunities to give my best to the world. So I began to say, "If life is a beach, then the opportunities of life are the oceans."

Have a wonderful week, Team!

Inspiration Action
Week 23 - Attitude

Write a thank you note to someone you know who generally has a good attitude day to day. Give the person a specific example of a time you noticed his or her good attitude in action. Document it here and include how it made the person feel and how it made you feel.

Best Monday Inspiration
Week 24 - Time

"Don't say you don't have enough time. You have exactly the same number of hours per day that were given to Helen Keller, Pasteur, Michelangelo, Mother Teresa, Leonardo da Vinci, Thomas Jefferson, and Albert Einstein."
- H. Jackson Brown

To help you with your time, there is no expounding this week!

Have a wonderful week, Team!

Inspiration Action
Week 24 - Time

Find a way to **make yourself take the time** to do something that you have been putting off for a while or perhaps take the first step or next step to get it done. Write what it is, write your progress on it at the end of the week, and write how you feel about your progress.

Best Monday Inspiration
Week 25 - Choices

"The only way to keep your health is to eat what you don't want, drink what you don't like, and do what you'd rather not."
- Mark Twain

This may not seem "inspirational," but it takes a pragmatic look at the choices that must be made sometimes in order to be your best. Although it is referring to health, of course it refers to any pursuit of high success. Looking at it on the flipside: The many ways to lose your health are to eat what you want, drink what you want, and do whatever you want to do.

With those two ways of looking at it, hopefully, inspiration to be and feel your best arrives when thinking about the results that are achieved and the additional self-empowerment that comes from making those tough choices time after time. Dessert or no dessert? Fried or baked? Exercise or no exercise? Wellness or sickness? The power to choose is an amazing, powerful, life-changing thing. Exercise your power to choose to be your best!

Have a wonderful week, Team!

Inspiration Action
Week 25 - Choices

Being your best includes having a healthy body that is fueled to help you do and be the things that you desire to do and be. This week's inspiration actions are health related, but the main point is to focus on being aware of how your choices impact your ability to be your best.

- Read an article about healthy food choices this week.
- Eat one less unhealthy item.
- Eat one additional healthy item.
- Write down the choices you made. Write about how you felt about making those choices, and then write about the results of the choices you made.

Best Monday Inspiration
Week 26 - Subconscious Snack

Inspiration must also operate at the subconscious level. Here is a subconscious snack consisting of inspirational words designed to help you think positively. Read each word and let it sink in by feeling the positive emotions related to each word.

Revitalized	Recharged	Dynamic	Cheerful	Rejuvenated
Purposeful	Adventurous	Dedicated	Inspired	Well-Informed
Committed	Responsible	Evolving	Devoted	Compassionate
Progressive	Confident	Enthusiastic	Optimistic	Well-Planned
Tenacious	Persistent	Innovative	Motivated	Self-Directed
Engaged	Determined	Diligent	Excited	Interdependent
Proactive	Appreciative	Foresightful	Creative	Well-Rounded
Methodical	Productive	Prepared	Focused	Results-Oriented
Supportive	Balanced	Disciplined	Eager	Self-Governed
Respectful	Cooperative	Inspiring	Driven	Principle-Based
Facilitative	Empowering	Contributive	Articulate	Unstoppable
Systematic	Thorough	Efficient	Prompt	Self-Assured
Organized	Meticulous	Industrious	Orderly	Completion
Undaunted	Considerate	Attentive	Prolific	Action-oriented
Accountable	Resourceful	Courageous	Positive	Collaborative

Wasn't that absolutely mentally yummy!!!

Have a wonderful week, Team!

Inspiration Action
Week 26 - Subconscious Snack

Pick ten words from the list that inspire you to work toward your best.

Write and post them somewhere for you to read daily for the rest of the week. Try to read them at least once in the morning and at least once in the evening. Feel the positive emotions of the words and let that positive emotion drive your thought process.

Best Monday Inspiration
Week 27 - Freedom

"Freedom is nothing but a chance to be better."
- Albert Camus

Withholding freedom from another human being is usually an attempt to keep that person suppressed enough to prevent him or her from reaching his or her potential. This motive is usually driven by a fear of an oppressed human being becoming better or more powerful than his oppressor; therefore, some type of force is used to keep the oppressed person from freely exercising all of the person's capabilities.

Let's take advantage of the freedom we have to exercise all of our capabilities. The most binding restraints we have as adults in modern society are those that we put upon ourselves. The most common personal restraints that we experience are the bondages of disbelief and emotional pain. No one but you can give you true lasting freedom from these two restraints. We can free ourselves from these restraints and with that freedom, give ourselves a wide-open chance to be better and ultimately **the best**.

Have a wonderful week, Team!

Inspiration Action
Week 27 - Freedom

Pick one thing that you and a team member at work can do together to be better or make better. Discuss with your team member and write the results of the discussion.

Pick one thing that you and a household member can enjoyably achieve together. Discuss with your household member and write the results of the discussion. If you are the only person in your household, you can do this with a friend or family member.

Best Monday Inspiration
Week 28 - Best Work

"Now is the accepted time, not tomorrow, not some more convenient season. It is today that **our best work can be done** and not some future day or future year. It is today that we fit ourselves for the greater usefulness of tomorrow. Today is the seed time, now are the hours of work, and tomorrow comes the harvest and the playtime."
- W.E.B. Du Bois

Your best can't wait another day. No delays, no hesitation. Let today, this week, be a step in the triumphant march toward being your best!

Have a wonderful week, Team!

Inspiration Action
Week 28 - Best Work

Look at the routine things you do this week, and find ways to do them better—not only once, but to make them better and keep them at that new level ongoing. Specifically, choose something in which you can make a difference in seven days. It can be something as simple as how you organize your shoes. (Ok, that might not be so simple for some, but you get the point!)

List two or three routine things and write about your efforts to do them better.

Best Monday Inspiration
Week 29 - Motivation

"People often say that **motivation** doesn't last. Well, neither does bathing – that's why we recommend it daily."
- Zig Ziglar

How do you motivate yourself? Even more importantly, on what motivation strategy do you rely when you need motivation? When things look their darkest, how do you positively reinforce your determination to succeed? How do you motivate yourself to perform the action that at first appears to be something you cannot do?

Motivation that propels you forward requires predictability and timing. Knowing a specific experience that you can purposefully take yourself through when you are de-motivated can help you through the toughest times. Remembering to use the strategy at the right times is also key. Having a dependable motivating stimulus can also train your brain to produce the right motivating hormones when you have a reliable motivate-me strategy or strategies.

For example, having a special song to listen to, or a story to read, or even learning something new when you sense a feeling of defeat, failure, or depression, can all tell your brain: "It's going to be ok. We'll make it and achieve it." When you read that story or listen to that song or experience the exhilarating insight of learning something new, your brain will produce hormones that positively affect your thoughts and body.

Best Monday Inspiration
Week 29 - Motivation

On the proactive side, according to Mr. Ziglar, motivating yourself daily is recommended. Motivation applied toward reaching your goals and dreams should be done regularly to help you stay energized and focused on your vision. It's easy to forget to motivate yourself with so much going on in life and most efforts being driven by the motivation to keep the bills paid. Remember to do things that keep you encouraged and pushing yourself forward to achieve those things that matter to you the most.

Have a wonderful week, Team!

Inspiration Action
Week 29 - Motivation

Write down three things that have motivated you in the past.

If you can't think of anything from the past, look around for personal or global current events, people, and situations to find some positive element (not including food or drink) to spur motivation.

Select 1 motivator that you can use the next time you feel defeated.

Look for opportunities this week to motivate others when they are feeling defeated. Write what you did and how it made you and the others feel.

Best Monday Inspiration
Week 30 - Make the Best Me

"As human beings, our greatness is not so much in being able to remake the world ... as in being able to remake ourselves."
- Mahatma Gandhi

We sometimes hear "make it a great day!" but, how about "make me a great me!" or "I'm going to make the **best me** I can." Even further, "I decide today to remake myself into my **best self**, regardless of any faults or failures of the past or fears of the future. I can and will consciously and purposefully define and make the **best me** that I can, starting today."

Have a wonderful week, Team!

Inspiration Action
Week 30 - Make the Best Me

List three important things you would like to better about yourself.

List three not so important things you would like to better about yourself.

Pick one item from each of the lists above. Observe your behaviors in these two areas over the next 4 days. Write about the behaviors you observed and the thoughts driving the behaviors. Identify and write new thoughts that are better aligned with improving in the two things you listed.

For the next three days, apply the new thoughts. Imagine yourself being better in the two things you listed. Concentrate your thoughts on what being better in those two things looks like and feels like.

Best Monday Inspiration
Week 31 - Enemies

"Am I not destroying my enemies when I make friends of them?"
- Abraham Lincoln

In today's world, some may cry malarkey on this strategy. However, if you want to make the world the best place it can be, this quote is a great way to start. It takes a lot of guts to pursue this strategy and a lot of pride swallowing, but you will be a double victor here as an enemy is defeated and a friend is gained all in one swing.

Have a wonderful week, Team!

Inspiration Action
Week 31 - Enemies

If you are in a challenging situation with another person (at work, school, home, store, anywhere) this week, step away from the situation for a period of time and later give the person a compliment about something he or she does well. It should not be about a physical trait or appearance; instead, make it about something specific that he or she does such as a skill or task. Write about what happens as a result of the compliment and how you felt about what happened.

Best Monday Inspiration
Week 32 - Who You Are

"The ultimate creative capacity of **your brain** may be, for all practical purposes, **infinite**."
- DRW Ross Adley - Brain Research Institute UCLA

"When you are looking in the mirror, you are looking at the problem. But, remember, **you are** also looking at **the solution**."
- Anonymous

"There is no satisfaction that can compare with looking back across the years and finding you've grown in **self-control, judgment, generosity, and unselfishness**."
- Ella Wheeler Wilcox

Knowing who you are today, **why you are** the way that you are today, and **who you can be** tomorrow are what these quotes are about. **Self-awareness**, or knowing why you say what you say and why you do what you do, is among the most valuable achievements you can pursue. Seeking the answers to those two questions can put you on a path of self-discovery that goes into deeply hidden thoughts that may be causing you delays in obtaining your full greatness. Accurately answering these questions about yourself can also be the catalyst for obtaining a purposeful, lasting, and graceful greatness that impacts your life and the lives of those around you.

Best Monday Inspiration
Week 32 - Who You Are

Don't just be you, be a great you and be purposefully and **gracefully** greater every day.

Have a wonderful week, Team!

Inspiration Action
Week 32 - Who You Are

Find and read an article or watch a video related to the book *The Emotional Life of Your Brain* by Richard J. Davidson. Write your thoughts about anything new you learned about your brain and your emotions from reading the article or watching the video.

Best Monday Inspiration
Week 33 - Acronyms

Here's a different inspiration to start this week. This list of acronyms represents ideas that we should be mindful of as we pursue our best. There are also a few listed just for a few laughs.

AAA
Alive, Alert, Aggressive
ABCD
Above and Beyond the Call of Duty
ADIDAS
All Day I Dream About Success
AFLO
Another Fantastic Learning Opportunity
ALF
Always Listen First
ASK
Activity, Skills, Knowledge
DRAW
Dignity and Respect At Work
DRIVE
Define, Review, Identify, Verify, Execute
ESO
Equipment Superior to Operator
FOBIO
Frequently Outwitted By Inanimate Objects

Best Monday Inspiration
Week 33 - Acronyms

GROW

Goals, Reality, Options, Will

PRIDE

Personal Responsibility In Delivering Excellence

SUCCESS

Sense of direction, Understanding, Courage, Charity, Esteem, Self-confidence, Self-acceptance (From Maxwell Maltz, Author of Psycho-Cybernetics)

CUOA

Compulsive Use Of Acronyms

AAAA

Association Against Acronym Abuse

Have a wonderful week, Team!

Inspiration Action
Week 33 - Acronyms

This week, be inspired by making someone smile. You can share this with someone to spread cheer or some other humorous and uplifting content. Write about the content you shared and how it felt to share a lighthearted, uplifting moment with someone.

Best Monday Inspiration
Week 34 - Listening

"To **listen** well is as powerful a means of **communication** and influence as to talk well."
- John Marshall

"The most basic and powerful way to connect to another person is to **listen**. Just listen. Perhaps the most important thing we ever give each other is our attention .... a loving silence often has far more power to heal and to connect than the most well-intentioned words."
- Rachel Naomi Remen

The tricky part about listening is trying to listen to someone who is not listening to you. This can create significant frustration. Therefore, listening is not just about listening, but it is also about patience. Going through the necessary dialogue and self-restraint to hear and understand what others are saying is not easy. I don't know if it ever gets easy, as our self-defense mechanisms are triggered anytime we feel unheard, or we feel misunderstood, or that our concerns are not being addressed the way we want them to be.

Best Monday Inspiration
Week 34 - Listening

Sometimes we find ourselves in a relentless pursuit to be understood. However, it is still critical to exercise productive and patient listening in even the most difficult conversations. Listening does not equate to conforming or agreeing. Listening should produce an understanding or a healthy recognition of not understanding. Good listening will contribute to continued healthy dialogue. Simply allowing someone to finish what they are saying can go a long way in creating working partnerships. While Q-Tips are good for hearing, patience is the tool of choice for good listening.

Have a wonderful week, Team!

Inspiration Action
Week 34 - Listening

1. Participate in a conversation with three or more people that lasts at least 5 to 10 minutes or longer. Count how many times someone gets cut off before they finish speaking. After the session, ask someone who was cut off, "How did it feel to keep getting cut off?"

2. Participate in another conversation and make it a point to continuously listen and do not respond until a person has clearly said everything they want to say. After the conversation ends, ask that person, "Do you feel like I was listening?"

Write your findings from these tests and your thoughts and feelings about what you learned.

Best Monday Inspiration
Week 35 - Infrastructure

"Letting your customers set your standards is a dangerous game because the race to the bottom is pretty easy to win. **Setting** your own **standards,** and living up to them, is a better way to profit. Not to mention a better way to make your day worth all the effort you put into it."
- Seth Godin

Setting up standards, processes, and new ways of thinking and operating may seem like a lot of work and even overkill or unnecessary at times. An infrastructure of best-of-breed options and procedures, however, must be developed and implemented to efficiently produce the best for customers, household members, club members, etc. Creating a strong infrastructure isn't easy and doesn't happen overnight, but it is necessary for long-term consistent success. As you move closer to developing a better infrastructure, be ready for change and sometimes seemingly extraneous work, but also be ready for the payoff of **being** considered **the best** in what you are doing.

Have a wonderful week, Team!

Inspiration Action
Week 35 - Infrastructure

1. List three things that occur repeatedly or regularly in your business, club, home, or group, that cause issues for the employees, club members, household members, group members, or customers.

2. If applicable, list three important tasks in your business that do not have a documented performance standard.

3. Analyze the items above to determine how they can be improved with consistent, thorough ways of doing them.

Examples: If you frequently receive requests from other departments to perform specific tasks and there is no standard, consistent way to handle the requests, resulting in issues for the groups involved—this would be an item to list and begin analyzing how it can be handled in a consistent way that reduces or eliminates errors and issues.

An example for home could be as simple as handling the mail. Does finding mail become a treasure hunt? Perhaps processing mail at home is an item to analyze within your household infrastructure.

Best Monday Inspiration
Week 36 - Publishing

"There's nothing to **writing**. All you do is sit down at a typewriter and open a vein."

- Walter Wellesley Smith

I think Mr. Smith is referring to the "pouring out of your blood" that seems to take place when writing something that is valuable to you. I'd like to steer this inspiration towards the topic of publications. Since it's probably fair to say that you have shed your own amount of blood in whatever work you do, you may have some great experiences and learning to draw from to publish articles. Credibility in being the best is strengthened by being published. You don't have to start by aiming for national syndication. Start with industry publications or even community periodicals.

Start putting your thoughts together about topics that you find helpful. Document your experiences and knowledge and share it with the public, such as a community newspaper, website, blog, social-media, or other communication outlets. Why? Sharing valuable information is a great way to help others pursue being their best and by helping others pursue their best, you help make the world a better place.

Have a wonderful week, Team!

Inspiration Action
Week 36 - Publishing

Pick a topic that you are interested in. Do a little research on 2 or 3 specific areas of the topic. After you've done a little research, write a page (about 300 words), or more if you like, about your topic.

After you've completed writing the paper, give it to two people you trust and ask them to read it. Ask them to ask you questions about the content to test your knowledge. Also, tell them that you are not asking for a writing critique and that you are only asking for an acknowledgment from them that you have completed the assignment of "publishing a paper". Regardless of what they say, reward yourself for completing this assignment.

Best Monday Inspiration
Week 37 - No Limits

"There are those that look at things the way they are, and ask why? I **dream of things that never were**, and ask why not."
- Robert F. Kennedy

"Man, alone, has the power to **transform** his **thoughts into physical reality**; man, alone, can dream and make his dreams come true."
- Napoleon Hill

I don't know if the part about "man, alone" is true because beavers seem to be able to transform thoughts about stopping water into reality by building dams, and lions seem quite capable of transforming their thoughts about dinner into reality by capturing their prey. However, Mr. Hill brings up a valid point about man's **superior** and almost **infinite** ability to transform thoughts into reality.

As we continue to consume the message of transforming our team and ourselves into our best, let's set no limits on what we can do!

Have a wonderful week, Team!

Inspiration Action
Week 37 - No Limits

Find and read an article about someone who went beyond his or her limitations and share the story with your team, family, club, or group. Write a few sentences about the article, write whom you shared it with, and the results of the sharing.

Best Monday Inspiration
Week 38 - Core Message

"**Making the beginning** is one-third of the work."
- Irish Proverb

"All glory comes from **daring to begin**."
- Eugene F. Ware

One significant shift forward on the road to being your best is daring to begin a new way of thinking. There comes a time when, as a team, we must end the old way of thinking and operating and **dare to begin a new way of thinking and operating**.

How can a new way of thinking and operating be created and reinforced? By aligning what we do day by day with a **core message**.

What is a core message? A core message is what drives everything we do, how we think, what we produce, and how we produce it. It is also how we think about ourselves as a group and how we interact with each other and those we serve. Our core message drives us to generate energy and produce efforts to be the best.

Best Monday Inspiration
Week 38 - Core Message

Our **Best Monday Inspiration Team** core message is:

Best Self ➡ **Best Team** ➡ **Best World**

Best Self represents each individual working to create the best self that he or she can create, leveraging strengths to positively impact others and understanding his or her individual challenges in order to transition from challenges to new strengths.

Best Team represents strategically developing a team that works well together. This best-team mentality should be recognizable to those who interact with you. It also represents having agreements on how you work together and agreements on what helps your team be the best team that you can be. A team may be your team at work, your family, club, civic group, or any other group of people working together.

Best World represents our intent to positively impact the world and leave the best legacy we can. It is our best selves working with our best teams to make the world a better place. The world may be your community, workplace, city, state, or country.

Best Monday Inspiration
Week 38 - Core Message

With **Best Self** ➡ **Best Team** ➡ **Best World** as our core message, we'll have a guide when making daily decisions.

When making decisions this week, ask yourself:
Is the decision I'm about to make helping me be my **best self**?
Is it helping our team, family, or group be its best?
Is it making a positive impact on the world around me?
Is it helping me leave a positive legacy for my family, community, workplace, city, state, or country?

Work with your team members to define how you want to have the greatest positive impact on your organization. Create something physical and visible that reminds the team of what the core message is. It could be something as simple as a poster board with cutout graphics and your message. It could be as elaborate as professional signage. Most importantly, it should represent what the group has agreed upon to be the core message and it should be enjoyable and encouraging for everyone to look at as a reminder of the core message.

For further reading on core messages, check out the book *Made to Stick* (Heath, Chip and Dan, 2007).

Have a wonderful week, Team!

Inspiration Action
Week 38 - Core Message

Create a core message for yourself. Your core message will drive everything you do, how you think, what you produce in the world, and how you produce it. It will be your measuring stick for making decisions.

If your team does not have a core message, bring up the idea for discussion.

Best Monday Inspiration
Week 39 - Detours

"Perseverance is getting back on track when you hit a detour."
- Catherine Pulsifer

Compare Ms. Pulsifer's explanation of perseverance to the following news story passage:

"Since a car bomb blinded Capt. Scott Smiley in Iraq, he has skied Vail, climbed Mount Rainier, earned his MBA, raised two young boys with his wife, won an Espy award and pulled himself up from faith-shaking depths."
- Michael Hill, Associated Press Writer – Fri May 21, 2010

These are activities that Capt. Smiley always wanted to do before his eyesight was instantly taken from him. After flatlining on a hospital bed, it is an enormous understatement to say that he simply hit a detour. However, he still got back on track and continued to achieve his desires.

It's real-life stories like this that make me refuse to give up. Allow Capt. Smiley's story to inspire you to be and produce **the best** that you can this week no matter what detours appear.

Have a wonderful week, Team!

Inspiration Action
Week 39 - Detours

Find and read an article about someone who should have given up but persevered despite the odds. Share that person's story with your team, family, club, or group.

Write a few sentences about the article you chose and the results of sharing it.

Best Monday Inspiration
Week 40 - Free Time

"The ultimate test for the ability to control the quality of experience is what a person does in solitude, with no external demands to give structure to attention. To fill free time with activities that require concentration, that increase skills, that lead to a **development of the self**, is not the same as killing time by watching television."
- Mihaly Csikszentmihalyi, From his book *Flow: The Psychology of Optimal Experience*

Pursuing your best requires making the best choices on how you spend your time. While it is not suggested that every second should be spent with your absolute strongest efforts of maximum productivity, it is suggested that you evaluate your activities on a regular basis to make sure you are making the best use of your time based on the goals you want to achieve.

Have a wonderful week, Team!

Inspiration Action
Week 40 - Free Time

If you have any free time this week, fill it with something new and/or productive. Write what you did, how you felt about doing it, and—of course—the results.

Best Monday Inspiration
Week 41 - Trauma

"Trauma—the root of all evil"
- Andrew Scheim

Today's inspiration might get into your personal business, but when I found this quote, I had to share it because it summarized perfectly the observations that I've made about barriers to **human potential**. Nature versus nurture is a standard discussion regarding what drives individual human behavior. While I'm not attempting to start a debate over cause and effect, I will share that I'm convinced that nurture plays an overwhelming part in how human beings individually respond to the world. When I closely watch the patterns of individuals' uncontrolled responses to stimuli, especially my own, I continuously see the patterns of how default responses tie back to categories of previous trauma. Trauma doesn't always equate to the presence of something severe in a person's past. Sometimes it is the lack of human needs being met, both while growing up and during adulthood.

Therefore, regarding you and your human potential and your path to your best self, what connections can you make between your past experiences and your current barriers, current fears, current episodes of unhappiness, and current anxieties and compulsions? More importantly, are you purposefully addressing these (the current issues and the past experiences) with perseverance and determination so you can pursue your Best Self?

Best Monday Inspiration
Week 41 - Trauma

I'm not talking about simply coping with your issues or simply resolving them. I'm talking about dogmatically identifying barriers in your life, obliterating them (after taking any good lessons learned from them), and creating strength and power where weaknesses and shortcomings once lived.

My closing thought is this: If trauma is the root of all evil then healing from trauma is the root of all compassion and success, which are key attributes of your **best self.**

Have a wonderful week, Team!

Inspiration Action
Week 41 - Trauma

Identify two traumatic experiences in your life. It could be a bad relationship or the loss of a job or house. It could be something in your childhood or young adult years. It could be the memory of someone shouting profanely at you while driving down the street. It could be a horrible customer service experience. It could be anything that has left an emotionally bad taste in your mouth.

Write down your two traumatic events and how they made you feel. Share them with someone that you trust. Determine if the traumatic events are in any way preventing you from being your best and if you may need to consider seeking help to address the trauma.

Best Monday Inspiration
Week 42 - Optimism

Promise Yourself

To be so strong that nothing can disturb your peace of mind.

To talk health, happiness, and prosperity to every person you meet.

To make all your friends feel that there is something in them.

To look at the sunny side of everything and make your optimism come true.

To **think** only **the best**, to **work** only for **the best**, and to **expect only the best**.

To be just as enthusiastic about the success of others as you are about your own.

To forget the mistakes of the past and press on to the greater achievements of the future.

To wear a cheerful countenance at all times and give every living creature you meet a smile.

To give so much time to the improvement of yourself that you have no time to criticize others.

To be too large for worry, too noble for anger, too strong for fear, and too happy to permit the presence of trouble.

To think well of yourself and to proclaim this fact to the world, not in loud words but great deeds.

To live in faith that the whole world is on your side so long as you are **true to the best that is in you.**

- Christian D. Larson

Best Monday Inspiration
Week 42 - Optimism

There's a lot of optimistic thinking in this promise! Even thinking half of these thoughts half of the time could certainly create a huge amount of new, life-giving, positive energy in an individual's world and propel one to be **the best**. It could also impact people nearby and create more positivity in their lives. Then, what if those impacted people caught on and exercised only this creed, creating a snowball effect of people optimistically creating their **best selves**, and this message continues to spread and grow from person to person? It could be life changing! It could be world changing! It could lead to having the **Best Team** and the **Best World** ever!

Have a wonderful week, Team!

Inspiration Action
Week 42 - Optimism

Read Christian D. Larson's promise to yourself every day this week.

Best Monday Inspiration

Week 43 - The Best

YOU
ARE
THE
BEST

Have a wonderful week, Team!

Inspiration Action
Week 43 - The Best

Every day this week...

- Tell yourself that you are **The Best**.
- Tell your household members that they are **The Best**.
- Tell your individual team members that they are **The Best**.
- No need to write about it. Only focus on doing it and enjoying the process of doing it.

Best Monday Inspiration
Week 44 - The Race

"If you set a goal for yourself and are able to achieve it, you have won your race. Your goal can be to come in first, to improve your performance, or just finish the race. It's up to you."
- Dave Scott, six-time Ironman Triathlon World Champion

The Ironman Triathlon requires contestants to persevere through a 2.4-mile swim in deep waters, a 112-mile bike up and down grueling hills in the blazing sun, and a 26.2-mile marathon. These are back to back feats of endurance that require one to dig down deep and tap into her or his potential. Not only did Mr. Scott train physically and prepare mentally to go from desire to being at the starting line, he also crossed the finish line in first place six times, earning his place in world history by giving his best.

Let this Ironman accomplishment inspire you to start and finish your own races of challenge, opportunity, and the race of reaching the potential that is in your life. Sometimes the toughest race to run is the race against self. To "just finish" the race against self can change your life tremendously.

Run your race with the determination to be your best.

Have a wonderful week, Team!

Inspiration Action
Week 44 - The Race

Look for opportunities to get stronger at something this week. Pick from one of the following categories:

- Eating healthy
- Responding controlled and strategically to challenges instead of reacting with stress
- Having conversations with new people that you would have normally avoided
- Exercising
- Listening
- Helping others

Write down what you chose. At the end of the week, write about how you felt about "the race" you ran to accomplish becoming stronger in what you chose.

Best Monday Inspiration
Week 45 - Learning

"Learning never exhausts the mind."
- Leonardo da Vinci

How times have changed. I would like to see Mr. Vinci sit through a modern-day eight-hour training session. Those can be quite exhausting.

Actually, I see the truth of his statement in this regard: Learning related to something that you are passionate about is inexhaustible because you want to know more and more about how to perform your craft better or to reach your goals. If you are not passionately learning more about what you do, perhaps your learning resources need to change or you may need to think about what you do. It may be time to change to doing something different.

May your learning (and application of what you learn) be inexhaustible as you continue toward being your best!

Have a wonderful week, Team!

Inspiration Action
Week 45 - Learning

Learn something new regarding your work, family, community, sports team, or club and share what you learned with that group this week.

Write what you learned, how you felt about learning it, and the results of sharing it with others.

Best Monday Inspiration
Week 46 - You Can

"The positive thinker sees the invisible, feels the intangible, and achieves the impossible."
- Winston Churchill

Yes, you can see the invisible (those possibilities that others refuse to see). You can feel the intangible (the inner knowing and energy of those possibilities that others don't sense), and you can achieve the impossible (what others are afraid to pursue).

Your positive thinking is a key to doing amazing things that others can't comprehend. Something may be as clear as day to you, but to others, it may be ridiculously unfathomable. Keep taking action while thinking positively and those things that you see and imagine will begin to move into reality. Know that you can do the things you think positively towards.

Have a wonderful week, Team!

Inspiration Action
Week 46 - You Can

This week, attempt to find something that isn't seen by others such as a potential problem or solution. If you usually see problems, try seeing a solution. If you usually only see solutions, try seeing a problem that hasn't been recognized yet. Remember, the goal is to break past the limitation of current thinking so you can focus on making things better. Write what you discovered and how it made you feel.

Best Monday Inspiration
Week 47 - Habits and Thoughts

"Powerful indeed is the empire of habit."
- Publilius Syrus

"Cultivate only the habits that you are willing should master you."
- Elbert Hubbard

By default, habits become a part of us through how we respond to experiences over time. Usually, when people talk about habits, they're referring to visible behaviors. However, let's look at the habit of *thought* because this is where the "powerful empire of habit" has its roots.

What are your thinking habits? Do you have a habit of being aware of your thoughts? Do you have a habit of controlling your thoughts or a habit of letting your thoughts control you? Can you *instantly* stop your thoughts in their tracks, analyze them, determine which are effective or noneffective, and then pursue or discard them appropriately? Can you discard those noneffective thoughts before they start a biochemical response and trigger negative chemical imprints in your brain? Can you consciously pursue your positive thoughts and allow positive chemical imprints in your brain to work in your favor?

Best Monday Inspiration
Week 47 - Habits and Thoughts

Your brain is structured to take your thoughts and perform amazing neural and chemical actions to respond and wire itself according to your thoughts.

Here's the good news. You have the power to choose. You can choose to develop habits for how you respond to your thoughts. While things outside of your control can trigger many of your thoughts, you can form habits for how you deal with those thoughts. **You can choose** to respond with productive, helpful thoughts that lead to encouragement and then deal with challenges in a real and productive way that uplifts you and those around you.

As we consider the purpose of **Best Monday Inspiration**—to change the way we think and operate as a team—it is critical to make consistent and purposeful efforts to follow thoughts that produce significantly positive energy and results. It is the habit of **Best Thoughts** that will lead to a habit of **Best Self**, **Best Team**, and **Best World**.

Have a wonderful week, Team!

Inspiration Action
Week 47 - Habits and Thoughts

1. List three habits you have successfully changed in your past.

2. List three habits you would like to change in your future.

3. List three new habits you would like to create.

Take steps towards #2, and #3 this week and make a plan to accomplish these changed/new habits in a specified period of time.

Best Monday Inspiration
Week 48 - Thank You

Please accept this week's **Best Monday Inspiration** as a sincere, personal **thank you** for investing your time, money, and mental and emotional energy into this workbook. Thank you for your decision and efforts to continue on the pathway toward being your best. Not only do I thank you, but the world thanks you because as you work to be and do your best, you make the world a better place.

I hope this week provides an opportunity for thankfulness at work and home. As life progresses, everyone has probably had something go wrong during this past year, whether it was minor or major. However, I hope that final tabulations show that more things have gone right than wrong in your life this past year. If by chance that does not turn out to be true, my hopes are for the next 12 months to be full of events going right for you.

Finally, thank you for being a part of the **Best Monday Inspiration Team** and any efforts you have done this year to add positive energy to the efforts of this publication. Thank you and congratulations to you for your pursuit to be your best!

Have a wonderful week, Team!

Inspiration Action
Week 48 - Thank You

Thank three people in your life for giving their best in whatever capacity you observed them doing so this year.

Write a note to yourself about four actions you performed your best at this year, regardless of the outcome. Thank yourself for giving your best.

Share your thank you inspiration actions on Facebook at facebook.com/bestmondayinspiration

Best Monday Inspiration
Week 49 - What a Ride

"Life should not be a journey to the grave with the intention of arriving safely in a pretty and well-preserved body, but rather to skid in broadside in a cloud of smoke, thoroughly used up, totally worn out, and loudly proclaiming, "Wow! What a Ride!"
- Hunter S. Thompson

Based on Mr. Thompson's well-documented personal matters we're going to redirect the author's possible original intent to suit the purpose of **Best Monday Inspiration**. I thought this quote was a passionate way to say: Find your purpose and then give it all you've got until there's no more to give. Don't leave anything on the table and give it your **best, all life long**!

Have a wonderful week, Team!

Inspiration Action
Week 49 - What a Ride

List #1. Write three major things you would like to accomplish in life that currently seem almost impossible right now.

List #2. Write three major things you would like your family to accomplish.

List #3. Write three major things you would like your team at work to accomplish.

Best Monday Inspiration
Week 50 - Dreams

"Dream lofty dreams, and as you dream, so shall you become. Your vision is the promise of what you shall at last unveil."
- John Ruskin

Is it a lofty dream to achieve national recognition as one of the **Best Teams** in your profession? Perhaps. Would you achieve that recognition accidentally? Probably not. What if your team had a unified vision of purposefully doing everything the team does the best way possible and had a vision of being nationally recognized as **The Best**? Would that create some type of synergy that propels the team closer and closer to national recognition? Mr. Ruskin and modern science say it could happen.

The human brain is engineered to work that way. Visions formed in the mind can spark neurological pattern-matching that subconsciously causes a human being to pursue things and objects. It also drives behaviors that match the vision that is fixed in the mind. So dream the lofty dream for everything you desire. As you do, add to your dreams a little advice from someone else.

"I would visualize things coming to me. It would just make me feel better. Visualization works if you work hard. That's the thing. You can't just visualize and go eat a sandwich."
- Jim Carrey

Have a wonderful week, Team!

Inspiration Action
Week 50 - Dreams

Take 1 item from each of the three lists you created from last week's inspiration action. This will be your list of 3 dreams that you'll pursue next year. For each dream, write 5 actions you can take to pursue the dream. Discuss each dream and each 5-action plan with someone you trust. After your discussion, apply any feedback as necessary and continue with your developing and executing the plans throughout the next year.

Best Monday Inspiration
Week 51 - Bunt or Out of the Park

"Don't bunt. Aim out of the ballpark."
-David Ogilvy

In baseball, the purpose of a bunt is to slightly hit the ball far enough (20 to 30 feet) so that a runner can advance to a base. The purpose of aiming out of the ballpark, of course, is to score one to four runs with one powerful swing of the bat.

As we look at our professional and personal goals, Mr. Ogilvy, a previous chairman of the largest marketing communications firm in the world says, in his own way, to not look at the safe, small advancing bunt-type goals. He suggests aiming to knock it out of the park. We understand that there are definitely times when we need to bunt, but for the purpose of inspiration, let's agree with Mr. Ogilvy, who seemed to practice what he preached by earning an induction into the Advertising Hall of Fame and by being known as the "Father of Advertising." Time magazine once called him "the most sought-after wizard in today's advertising industry." He also wrote a sales training manual that was considered to be the best available for almost 30 years.

Best Monday Inspiration
Week 51 - Bunt or Out of the Park

As you look at your individual goals in various parts of your life, ask yourself "Am I bunting or aiming out of the park? If I'm bunting, why am I bunting?" Being deeply introspective with your answers will reveal the need for increasing your skill and power for knocking it out of the park.

I look forward to hearing your success stories (both home runs and bunts) through the next year.

Share your stories on Facebook at
facebook.com/bestmondayinspiration
Have a wonderful week, Team!

Inspiration Action
Week 51 - Bunt or Out of the Park

Look at three areas of your life and ask yourself, "Am I bunting or swinging out of the park? Why?" Write down these areas and your responses.

Area 1

Area 2

Area 3

Inspiration Action
Week 51 - Bunt or Out of the Park

If any of the three areas are being driven by fear, make a decision to implement a bunt or out-of-the-park strategy based on a determination to be your best, rather than on fear. Begin this strategy by documenting your findings and decisions here and how you feel about your findings.

Best Monday Inspiration
Week 52 - Lifelong Determination

"Strange is our situation here upon earth. Each of us comes for a short visit, not knowing why, yet sometimes seemingly to a divine purpose. From the standpoint of daily life, however, there is one thing we do know: That we are here for the sake of others…for the countless unknown souls with whose fate we are connected by a bond of sympathy. Many times a day, I realize how much my outer and inner life is built upon the labors of people, both living and dead, and how earnestly I must exert myself in order to give in return as much as I have received."
- Albert Einstein

Some of what we enjoy in our lives is due to others (some still present and some long gone) who gave their **best**. Let us do the same for the families, jobs, communities, all those we serve, and those who come after we're long gone. Let us wrap up this 52-week journey with a lifelong determination to be the best we can be and may those we serve remember our labor as being some of the **best** ever seen.

Have a wonderful week, Team!

Inspiration Action
Week 52 – Lifelong Determination

Write your most valuable experiences and most memorable thoughts that you had from 52 weeks of **Best Monday Inspiration**. Share with others and pass the inspiration along.

Share your final inspiration actions on Facebook at facebook.com/bestmondayinspiration

The Best Thank you!

You bought the book. Thank you!

You stuck with it through all 52 weeks. Thank you!

Perhaps you've shared **Best Monday Inspiration** with someone else. Thank you!

If you have expressed any positive thoughts towards **Best Monday Inspiration**, thank you!

With modern life containing so many opportunities to focus on other things, it is with great gratitude that I express thanks to you for taking your time to read and participate in **Best Monday Inspiration**.

You are **The Best**.

www.ingramcontent.com/pod-product-compliance
Lightning Source LLC
LaVergne TN
LVHW051559070426
835507LV00021B/2655